Hungry People

feeding your folks during a global pandemic

Camille Coleman

Y'all...eggs + cheese + random junk in your fridge...it's your ticket to culinary rock-stardom with your hungry people. AND you get to be all Earth friendly and stuff by recycling what you already have. 1. Grab your shady veggies and whatever (I had spinach, red onion, and sausage) and sauté it until it gets itself right with the world. 2. Take out your frustrations on some egg whites with a whisk. This is no time for a hand mixer. We need to emote here. Add the yolks and whatever seasonings tickle your fancy. 3. Slap those fluffy eggs in your pan and let them set up a bit and get right with the world, too. 4. Add yo junk. And a healthy amount of cheese. Because calcium. 5. Flop that sucker in half to get that calcium to melting and slide onto your plate. Paper is perfectly acceptable in these times-we're not here to judge. If you're into it, salsa that baby up. 6. Get your 8 x 10 glossy publicity photos and a sharpie ready, because you're going to be signing some autographs. 7. Retire to the comfy spot of your choice and let your people do the dishes. Because rock stars don't do dishes.

Since I'm being food-bossy, eat you some protein. Like, steak. No grill? No prob. Sear your seasoned meats in a screaming hot pan until it screams uncle. Or moo. Or whatever. Chuck some butter in there (again, yummy animal fats-don't judge) until it foams. Slip it into a preheated oven for a bit of you feel you must eat it medium well (sorry, y'all, I like mine "whiffed" by the fire-again, don't judge). Tomorrow, slice up those leftovers and chuck it on that bag of baby spinach that is crying out to be used before it gets blinky. Finally, tell your cat to keep her floofy mits off your deliciousness.

Today I found her lurking at the bottom of the produce bin. And because we are bound and determined to use ALL the fresh stuff first, it was time for this girl to take a trip to the spa-the sauna, to be precise. Preheat your oven to a screaming hot 400°, but be sure to remove the leftover cornbread you were storing in there first *ahem*. Peel her slightly and lop off her root. If she falls apart a little, cut her some slack. These are tough times. Tuck her into a foil nest and lube her up with some olive oil. Next, make her a hat. Bonus points for making it look like the Apollo 13 command module with panache. Let her roast for 40ish minutes at 375° until she is the golden bronze beauty she was meant to be. Slather that soft, nutty, sweet goodness on anything you can find. A baguette. Toast points. A flip flop. Whatever. My delivery device of choice was buttered penne with a splash of heavy cream and plenty of Parmesan, because we are using what we have on hand. And we believe in plenty of calcium. Finally, if you plan on quarantine canoodling, make sure you share. Because when it comes to onions and garlic, sharing is caring. Really.

For lunch, my take on panzanella salad. Because I'm down for any salad whose main ingredient is bread. A day old baguette is usually the way to go, but I went with cornbread, because leftovers. It's certainly NOT because I accidentally left it in the oven while preheating yesterday. Crumble that golden goodness in your bowl. Chop up a tomato, red onion, green onion, or any other kind of onion you have floating around and add them to the party. That garlic you roasted yesterday? She loves a good party, so chuck her in, too. Drizzle with a little olive oil and dust with a smidge of salt. And because we want strong bones and teeth, a healthy amount of Parmesan. Fluff up with a fork and feast! Then congratulate yourself on turning your leavings into culinary greatness.

Are your people hungry AGAIN? Sauté some onion and garlic in a smidge of butter and olive oil. Chuck in the dregs of the spinach sill pouting in the fridge. Rescuing a box from the freezer? Make sure to wring her out-she tends to get a little weepy in recipes and we don't need that kind of negativity in our lives. Drizzle in half and half or heavy cream until you feel good about yourself and your life choices. Add mounds and mounds of Parmesan because you know how we feel about healthy teeth and bones. Let it all bubble away until thick and ridiculously good. Next, make a divot for each egg and get cracking. Slip the whole kit and caboodle into a 350° oven for 15ish minutes or until the whites are no longer jiggly. Top with chives and more cheese if you're feeling fancy. Slide that skillet of goodness on the table, scoop some on your plate, and get back to binge watching The Crown. Then congratulate yourself on only having ONE pan to clean. Or for your people to clean. They'll thank you later.

Cousous salad. Yup, I know this one may sound a bit odd, but listen to me now and believe me later. My French host mom made it on the regular and if the French cook it or wear it, I want it. Couscous, hard boiled eggs, kalamata olives, tomato, and whatever else is pouting in your fridge (my chives and scallions were crying out to me). Drizzle with a few glugs of olive oil and dust with garlic salt. Feeling a bit more feisty? Use your favorite vinaigrette. Also, couscous is ridiculously easy and delicious. Never made it? Dump it in a bowl, add some boiling water from your kettle, cover for five minutes, et voilà! Fluff that gorgeousness and eat it with ALL your stuff. Easy peasy, and you will feel très fancy.

Sometimes ya girl just needs a steak and there's no better sidekick than a great baked potato. For years I just wadded them up in foil and chucked them in the oven for a bit or *gasp* let them spin in the microwave until they were somewhat edible. People, there is a better way. And the best part is that it takes no more time or effort, but yields a tuber that will make your eyes roll right back into your head. First, scrub 'em and jab 'em a few times with a knife so they don't explode. Next, lube them up with plenty of olive oil and roll those bad boys in PLENTY of salt. I like a course grind, but you do you. Pro tip: while your hands are oiled up and salty, take a minute to give yourself a mini-mani. Let's face it- our hands are taking a beating with all the washing, sanitizing and whatnot, so give them a little love and scrub away. Park those taters on a baking sheet and slide them into a 400º oven for AT LEAST an hour. That's it. There's nothing more to do, other than gussy them up with the toppings of your choice. The sky's the limit. In fact, slap the protein of your choice on there (hello, leftover meats of all descriptions) and you've got a complete meal in one tasty, fluffy, and ridiculously easy little package! Once you use this method, you'll never go back to your potato nuking ways. And you'll have the softest hands on the block. Win-win.

People, if you roast a chicken on Sunday, you'll be thanking yourself all week long. Deliciousness tonight, and great leavings to chow on later! My little lady came already spatchcocked, which is just fancy talk for "laid that girl out flat." It doesn't change how I dress her up to roast, but does cut down on the time she spends in the sauna. First, rinse her off and dab her dry with a paper towel. Then slip some sliced lemon, salt, and chopped garlic under her skin. Finally, schmear her down with butter and shake her down with some good onion salt (no one beats Trader Joe's). Slip her in a 350° sauna for about 35 minutes or until her skin looks like she's had a great day at the beach. Slide her on your cutting board and let her rest. Girlfriend has had a day. And don't even think about getting rid of those drippings- you know better than to waste perfectly good rendered fat. Feast on your bits of choice, then pick her clean and tuck all that glorious meat in the fridge for later. Take the carcass (skin, bones, and all) and dump it in a pot with the drippings, pouting veggies from the produce bin, and whatever herbs you have on hand. Let that concoction bubble away until your home smells like chicken heaven. After it cools, strain and pop that liquid gold in the fridge for later. Trust me. You'll be glad you did.

If you roast a chicken and have leftovers, you'd better believe you are in for some glorious chicken salad. There are exactly 8.4 billion variations on this theme but since the chicken is already loaded with flavor, I like to keep it simple. And unless you want a southern woman tsk tsking you, do NOT use any dark meat, bless your heart. Start by whirring a breast in your food processor using the pulse thingy. Over processing can lead to chicken paste, and chicken paste is exactly as tasty as it sounds. Dump that goodness in a bowl but for heaven's sake, don't wash out the processing bowl. We've got enough dishes in our sink already. Next, rescue your sad celery and green onions, chuck them in and whir them up until they are finely chopped. If they get a bit weepy, get all Tom Hanks on them and wring them out because, like baseball, there is no crying in chicken salad. Add them to your bowl with a couple of glops of mayonnaise. And by mayonnaise I mean Duke's or Hellmann's. Anything else will hurt that chicken's feelings. Hold off on the seasoning while you're at it. That roasted chicken is bringing all the good flavor, so you may not even need salt. Give 'er a taste and add accordingly. Of course I am pro-carb and love this on a good slab of sourdough, but I had some Campari tomatoes staring me down that wouldn't take no for an answer. Believe me, after using roasted chicken breast to make your salad, you'll never go back.

Confession: I have never been on a street in Mexico. In fact, everything I know about Mexican street corn I learned from Nacho Libre. I promise you, though, you will not swat these cobs outta yo face. First of all, march yourself right past the giant pile of ears that are four for a dollar and go STRAIGHT to the ones sold in fours under cellophane. They have never let me down in the sweet delicious goodness department. Boil those lovelies up, drain well, and line 'em up. Squeeze a couple of limes over them until they've given up every drop of their tart goodness. Shake a generous amount of Tajin on everyone (look for her in the spice aisle). Then shake your own groove thang because you can. Next, thin some sour cream with a little cream, half and half, or buttermilk (because we like it tangy) and drizzle away. Shake on more Tajin. Finally, grate generous heaps of Parmesan until they cry uncle. Then grate a little more. Feelin' extra sassy? Get to squeezing on a couple of extra lime wedges and dig in. Never mind this Mexican street corn is sitting on English transfer ware and topped with Italian cheese. I can think of no better way to celebrate humanity than to bring all the nations together on one delicious plate. Bon appétit, y'all!

Does someone need a hug? During these pandemic times, I'm pretty sure we all do, and a great bowl of tomato soup is like a big, warm, comforting hug from the inside out. Start by opening a big can of Cento crushed tomatoes and dump it in your saucepan. Anything other than Cento is a travesty, but pandemic times. I'll cut you some slack. Need to atone for the bag of cheese doodles you polished off last night (not that I would know)? Let's sneak some extra nutriments in there. Put your liquid chicken gold in the bullet-type device of your choice and whir it up with a couple of fists full of spinach. Yes, spinach. I promise you, your people will never know it's in there. Add your whirred mixture and a couple of dashes of salt to the saucepan and let it bubble away for a bit. Once it has thickened slightly, add a few glugs of milk, half and half, or heavy cream. Note: I listed them in ascending order of greatness, but use what you have. Let it bubble a little longer while you throw together a grilled cheese sandwich as the perfect delivery device. I went with fresh mozzarella because that's what I had and he was getting a little testy. Ladle that liquid hug in a bowl and, for crying out loud, top it with Parmesan to up the nutritional value of the whole thing. And the secret spinach thing? We'll just keep that between us.

People are getting hungry again, but today we get to enjoy the fruits of our labor earlier this week to feed the fruit of our loins. All we have to do is chop, chuck, and bubble. Chop your poutiest veggies, chuck in your pot with some liquid gold and leftover chicken, then let it bubble away with some egg noodles (or rice) from the pantry. Bam. Deliciousness. It's good for the soul, y'all. And you barely lifted a finger!

Y'all, I like big butts. I cannot lie. Pork butts, that is. Which isn't really a butt, but I guess that sounds more alluring than pork shoulder. And she becomes even more appealing when you plop her in a slow cooker for several hours. My little herb pot needed a haircut, so I tossed that in there, too, along with some red onions that were just hanging around. Low and slow is the name of the game, so let her hang out in there for several hours. The bad news is that you have to smell that deliciousness all. Day. Long. The good news is that you get to smell that deliciousness all. Day. Long. And once she is done, all you have to do is look at her sideways and she falls apart. If you poke her and she puts up a fight, close that lid and ignore her truculence a little while longer. Eventually she will give in. While you are waiting her out, use your potato baking skills as a delivery device for your pork. This time, though, try a sweet potato! Scrub, poke, slather, salt, and slide in a 400° oven for an hour. Since they have a higher sugar content, you may see some caramelized bits as it roasts, but don't panic. That's straight up yum. Slit that girl open, give her a dollop of sour cream (or Greek yogurt if that's what you've got), and pile on some of that glorious pork. That's it. Really. You don't need anything else. It's salty, it's sweet, it's creamy. What more could you want? And if that wasn't enough, you've got leftover pork for more goodness later this week. You and your people will love it. No lie.

Confession: I'm not a baker. Too much precision involved. In fact, I rely on Hungry Jack's buttermilk pancake mix for the bulk of my breakfast-carb needs. In my quest to use what I have, I figured out how to make a great delivery device for that pork we whipped up last night-a yummy drop biscuit, or a friend's granny called them, "a horny biscuit" (simma down, y'all-it's because it looks like a horny toad). Mix together two parts pancake mix, one part buttermilk or thinned sour cream, and a dribble of melted butter. Better yet, a dribble of the renderings of your pork. Mix until just combined, drop in biscuit-sized mounds on a greased baking tray, and slide into a 400° oven for 10ish minutes, or until that biscuit is golden and happy. Split that lovely open and pile on the pork. Have some cabbage? Quick-pickle it up and pile it on, too. Add a glass of sweet tea (the house wine of the south, y'all) and you are ready to dig into a yummy southern feast! It's slap yo mama good. But don't slap yo mama-we love our mamas. And you'll get grounded.

Got tomatoes? Fresh mozzarella? A generous basil plant named Basel? Then you are certified to go caprese crazy. And because we need to use all the fresh stuff first, it's totally ok to eat variations on this theme two meals in a row. In the first iteration I found some naan bread begging to be transformed into a gorgeous margherita flatbread. All you need is a drizzle of olive oil, slices of fresh tomato and mozzarella, and a dusting of sea salt. Hold off on the basil for now. Like me, he gets all sulky in high heat, so we'll add him later. Slide that beauty onto the rack (yes, straight on the rack) of a 400° oven for about 10 minutes. Meanwhile, sweetly ask Basel for a few leaves. He will gladly oblige. Stack those pretty leaves, roll into a tiny green cigar, and slice into ribbons (fancy folk call that a chiffonade) to sprinkle on top once she comes out of the oven, because who doesn't like a little extra. Devour immediately. For an encore, find some good crusty bread and get your grilled cheese on. Second verse, same as the first, but with sourdough. Feeling fancy? Add a drizzle of 18 year balsamic vinegar for good measure. And in both versions, make sure you give your sliced tomato a good dab, bless her. I believe in a good cry, but not on my sandwich. Or my flatbread. Get your crazy on, y'all, and your hungry people with thank you!

Popovers. Or as our friends across the pond call them, Yorkshire pudding. Little eggy puffs that dress up anything from a salad to a Sunday roast. They look fancy, but are super easy and will impress all your people. Start by cranking up the oven to 400°. Plop a knob of salted butter in each well of a muffin tin. You don't need a hoity popover pan, unless you just happen to have one in your butler's pantry. Slide the pan in the oven to melt the butter and heat up the pan (which is what makes all the magic happen because science and steam and stuff). Meanwhile, drop three eggs, a hefty pinch of salt, a cup of milk, and 3/4 cup of flour in a blender or smoothie bullet thingy. Whir it up until it is smooth and happy. Pull your hot pan out and fill each well halfway with the batter. Little brown bits? No worries, that is straight up browned butter goodness. Pop back into the oven, and in 11ish minutes pull out those bad boys and impress all your people with your baking wizardry. Serve immediately for maximum deliciousness. Slap on a little strawberry butter and you'll be transported right back to the café at Neiman's with your mama. Use a cast iron skillet and you've got yourself a German Pancake, which is the perfect delivery device for the berries of your choice. Breakfast magic, y'all. Add leftover sausage and you've got Toad in the Hole. I don't make up the names, folks, I just report the facts. Your people will love these, y'all, and that's a fact!

What's that? Your people are hollering for pizza? No problem, because we can take two ingredients we have on hand, throw in the dregs of what's in the produce bin, et voilà! Pizza! Mix together equal parts Greek yogurt and self-rising flour for the dough. Yup, that's it. No self rising flour? No problem. For every cup of flour add 1 1/2 teaspoons baking powder and 1/4 teaspoon salt. Bam. Self-rising flour. No Greek yogurt? I didn't have any either, so I used sour cream and it worked a treat!!! Mix until it's all crumbly, then get your freshly scrubbed hands in there and work it into a ball. Throw that ball on a floured board and knead a little. No need to go crazy. Divide that dough up, pass it out, and tell your people to get rolling and topping. Slide their mini masterpieces on a parchment lined baking tray for 12ish minutes at 425°. I went with a thin layer of Alfredo sauce topped with pouty spinach, garlic, and of course, Parmesan. I also had two jars of olives making googly eyes at me from the pantry shelf, so they joined the party, too. Finally, a thinly sliced pear topped with Gorgonzola. A moment of silence for the crazy deliciousness, please. Don't like a good stinky bleu? Creamy and salty Gruyère loves a sweet pear pairing, too. However you top it, you can't top a super quick, easy, and delicious crust. Now that your people are full and happy, you can get back to reading Love in the Time of Covid...errr..Cholera. Bon appétit, y'all!!

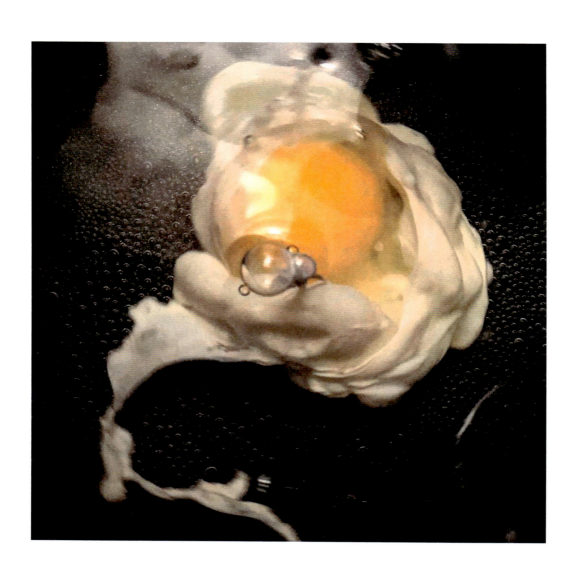

We are poaching eggs and we are kickin' it old school. Like, no special gadgets required. Why? Because 1. deliciousness and B. it's straight up scientiffery. That's right, get your kiddos in the kitchen/science lab for some fun with a side of chemistry and physics! Heck, let them come up with a hypothesis and stuff, then research why it is that this works. Begin with all your stuff "mise en place" which is fancy for "get all your stuff laid out and ready to go." This is a quick process and you'll want to be good to go. Lay out a clean towel, slotted spoon, and an egg cracked and ready. In a saucepan get your water up to a gentle simmer and add a glug of vinegar (chemistry, y'all). With a slotted spoon, get that hot tub swirling and drop your egg right into the middle of the action (physics, people). Once the white is set, fish her out with the slotted spoon and dab well, because watery is not delicious. Finally, plop that goodness on toast, eggs Benedict, a frisée salad, whatever. People, I believe that children are our future. Teach them well and let them FEED you. And keep them entertained during these covid times. Amen.

I needed a little pretty, healthy, AND delicious, and my freezer sweetly obliged. Pretty parcels of spinach and chèvre in phyllo dough. Thaw and wring out that spinach really well, because you know how we feel about tears in our food. Break up some herbed chèvre and add to your well-composed spinach. No goat cheese? Use the non-weepy cheese of your choice. Season that goodness up with some garlic salt and you are all set. Let your phyllo dough come to room temp and lay 3ish sheets of that gossamer loveliness on your board and cut into a square. Make sure to tuck the unused dough under a damp towel. Girl dries out quickly and gets all cranky and crumbly if you leave her hanging. Add a plop of that gorgeous mixture to the center, draw the four corners of your dough together, and twist into a little parcel. Give her a quick spritz of cooking spray and slide her into a 350º oven for about 10 minutes or until she is toasty and tanned. Serve those beauties up next to a gorgeous steak or at your next cocktail party. Très fancy, très delicious, and très easy. And if we ever needed a little of that, it's right now. Food can't fix all the sadness and frustration, but as I try to make sense of this and figure out how to use any bit of agency I may have to make someone else's life better, I'm looking for beauty in even the smallest of things. Let's listen. Let's learn. Let's feed and care for one another and do what we can to make the world a better place, y'all.

In France, it's not unusual to have cheese or fruit for dessert, so why not both at the same time? And when you've already got the grill fired up for your meats, you have the perfect scene for summer fruity cheesy goodness. Halve some nectarines, lube the cut side with a smidge of oil and slap those beauties on face down. Once they are a bit toasted, plop 'em on a platter, top with herbed chèvre (all hail the goat, y'all), drizzle on a bit o' honey, and dust with course salt. I had some fresh thyme (nectarines and thyme have been going steady for a long time) so I threw a little on, because fancy. And crazy delicious. Fast, easy, and fresh summer dessert that is guaranteed to make your eyes roll ALL the way back in your head, y'all.

One day a sweet little sweet potato found herself sitting next to a grater and, when their eyes met, they knew they were destined for grateness. Before she knew it she was peeled, blotted, and grated. All she needed was a little love, a tiny glug of oil, a dusting of salt, and a well-greased muffin tin to fulfill her destiny. Then things got hot and heavy in a 375° oven for 20 minutes. When she emerged, she knew that her beauty would only be enhanced by all of the things she could hold. An egg for breakfast. Barbecued chicken for lunch...the world was her oyster. She knew she wasn't relegated to the baking and mashing of her ancestors. With so many options before her, her story, and future greatness, continues. And all because of the love of a grater. The end.

Have you ever read the list of ingredients on a bottle of salad dressing? I'm pretty sure most of it comes from outer space, and we don't want to hurt our summer produce's feelings like that. Plus, whizzing together a vinaigrette is easier than you think! I use a 3:1 ratio of oil to vinegar, but you will discover what floats your boat. We are aiming for fat and acid, so use what you have. Does citrus juice count as an acid? Absolutely. And it's absolutely delicious. Put your oil and vinegar of choice in a blender or food processor and whir it up. Pro tip: a dab of Dijon mustard will add a little kick and keep the dressing emulsified and happy. Ok, here's where I may lose some of you, but listen to me now and believe me later-we are adding anchovies. Yes, those weird little fish that no one (except me) wants on their pizza. What they add is a savory, nutty deliciousness that will make your eyes roll all the way back. And I promise, never have I ever had someone taste my vinaigrette and say, "Excuse me, lady, did you pulverize some funky little fish in this concoction?" Not. Once. Toss in 3ish filets and give it another whir, a taste, and add salt and pepper as needed. Once you find your ratio, you can add all sorts of goodness to suit your salad. Minced shallots, fresh herbs, the sky's the limit. Not only will you feel all chefy making it, you can pronounce all the ingredients. And by all means, do not fear the fish. It will take your vinaigrette game to the next level. Bon appétit, y'all!

Y'all, it's HOT out there, so a cool salad that hits all the flavor profiles and textures is just the ticket, and today we're roasting beets to get us there. With all that rich and messy color we are guaranteed of two things: they are chock FULL of all sorts of phyto-goodness, and it's about to look like a bona fide crime scene up in here. I suggest you not wear your favorite silk blouse. I also suggest you spritz your cutting board with a little cooking spray to mitigate all the stainage and make clean up a snap. Peel and slice 'em, lube 'em up with good olive oil, dust with a little salt, and slide those ruby red beauties in a 400° oven for about 25 minutes. Let those girls cool down, plop 'em on a bed of spring greens, and top with a little chèvre (a moment of silence for the goat) and candied walnuts. With all this creamy, sweet, and earthy goodness, we don't need a full-fledged vinaigrette, just a dash of red wine vinegar to balance it all out. Happy roasting, y'all, and bon appétit!

The lovely eggplant. Isn't she a beauty, so sleek and curvy? Sadly she is holding on to some bitterness inside and we are here to help, but it's going to require a bit of tough love and getting a little salty with her. Peel her, slice her up, lay her out on paper towels, salt her down on both sides, and let her cry out her salty tears until she gives up all that bitterness, bless her. Lube her up with olive oil and lay that girl out on a hot grill until she is all smoky and sultry. Now our girl is soft, sweet, and ready for action. Whir her up with some olive oil, salt, lemon, garlic, tahini (that's sesame seed paste, y'all), and plenty of fresh parsley. Voilà! Baba ganoush! It's like hummus' smoky, sassy little cousin starring our girl eggplant rather than the chickpea. Fancy something a little more colorful? Serve her up with your favorite roasted veggies atop a fluffy bed of couscous and impress all of your hungry people. Either way, you'll sleep well tonight knowing that, because we showed her some love, she has become all she was meant to be. And more. Bon appétit, y'all!

Y'all, it's Friday, it's hot, and WE DO NOT COOK! We scrounge the fridge for all of this week's leavings, slap it on a board (because board=fancy) and tell our hungry people to have. At. It. Bon appétit, y'all.

Got some hungry people? A couple of eggs and some spaghetti? And just enough energy to boil some water? You're in luck, because that's all it takes for a delicious and filling carbonara. Chuck in a few extra staples and you elevate yourself to super fancy in a flash! While that spaghetti is bubbling away, whisk together two eggs, salt and pepper, grated Parmesan (because who are we to deny our teeth and bones some good nutrition), a bit of grated garlic, and chopped parsley if you have it on hand. Bonus points if you have some bacon to zuzsh it up a little. Once your spaghetti is al dente, grab those tongs and start loading it into your egg mixture. No need to even dirty up a colander! In fact, we want a little of that starchy water to keep everything loose and feeling good. Grab those tongs and get everyone well-aquatinted. The heat of the pasta water will cook the eggs and create a velvety sauce that will make you a quick-dinner hero. If the mixture gets a little too "tight" use a little more of your pasta water to loosen it up a bit. Heck, use some half and half if you're feeling sassy. Top all that goodness with an extra heap of Parmesan and present it to your hungry people post haste. This is best served right away. And all you had to do is crack some eggs and boil some water. Your people won't know how easy it was. And I'm not telling them otherwise. Bon appétit, y'all!

If you roast a chicken, then you must have some sort of potato to go with it, otherwise the universe might get all wonky and out of kilter. We could just chuck them in the roasting pan with our little lady, but sometimes our tubers need a little je ne sais quoi to delight us during these Covid times. Today we are going to squish 'em and roast 'em with plenty of butter and garlic. Not mash, not smash, but squish. Start by getting those lovelies (I like new potatoes best for this method) boiling in salted water. As they bubble away, grate up as much garlic as you dare and combine with a "healthy" amount of butter. Dust with a little salt and nuke that goodness for about 30 seconds or so. Prepare thyself- your home is about to smell like garlic heaven. Once your potatoes are fork tender, fish them out with tongs and let them drip dry on your cutting board for a minute. Next, plunk them on a baking sheet lined with parchment and get to squishing. I used a highball glass and it worked a treat, but use anything you have on hand that has a flat bottom. Next, spoon your glorious garlic butter over each one and slide into a screamin' hot 425º oven for about 15 minutes, or until they cry uncle and get all crispy around the edges. Gorgeous tuber goodness that is happy along side just about anything. Bon appétit, y'all!

If you are looking for another "clean out the fridge" delivery device, look no further than that pile of leftover rice crying out to you from the back of the fridge. That's right, leftover rice isn't just for pudding, y'all! Heat up a skillet with a dribble of veg oil and toss in your rice. Let her get her sizzle on for just a bit, then add whatever it is that you have pouting in the fridge (I happened to have sautéed mushrooms, scallions, and leftover chicken). Once everybody is feeling nice and toasty, make a well in the center of the skillet. Crack an egg right in the middle of the whole operation, let it set up a bit, then start swirling away to scramble her. Once she's ready to go, toss everyone together with a smidge of hoisin and a dribble of soy sauce. Top with more scallions and sesame seeds if you're feeling super fancy, et voila! Who'd have thought that a pile of rice and an egg could come together for such a quick and tasty supper for our hungry people? We did, because we are resourceful like that! As always, bon appétit, y'all!

I don't know about y'all, but when it's this hot, I need a cool salad to remind me that we all aren't about to spontaneously combust. In fact, having a couple of salads (chicken, tuna, pasta, whatever) ready to go in the fridge is a great way to stave off the mid-summer crankies. While your pasta is boiling away in well-salted water, mix up a simple vinaigrette in the bottom of a large serving bowl. I used red wine vinegar, olive oil, and a pinch of Greek seasoning, but whiz up the acid, oil, and seasonings of your choice. Drain, rinse, and dump it right in with your vinaigrette to let it soak up all the deliciousness. Next, chop up your favorite summertime bounty. I went with seeded tomato, cucumber, red onion, Greek olives, and a few sprigs of fresh oregano. Add them to the party, give it a good mix, and let them chill in the fridge for about 20 minutes to get all cozy with each other. Need to feel a little more righteous? Park your tasty salad on a bed of pretty greens and go to town. Oh, and the longer it sits in the fridge, the better it gets, so go ahead and make plenty for you and your hungry people to enjoy later. Trust me, we need all the help we can get to make sure cooler heads prevail in this heat, and this salad could very well save lives. Bon appétit, y'all!

I do love to eat lots of veggies, but on a Friday night, sometimes we just need all. The. Meats. And until I can have someone bring a sizzling skillet of fajitas right to my table, I'm going to do what I can here at home. Take a flank steak, trim her of excess fat and silvery membrane stuff, pat her dry and salt her down. If you have a meat tenderizer poky thing, then you are fancy. I'm not, so I just use the tip of my knife to poke her allll over. In a big zip-top bag or shallow casserole dish, combine soy sauce, fresh lime juice, and enough crushed garlic that you are in a certified vampire-free zone. Throw that steak into the marinade for a good meet-n-greet of at least an hour. Longer is better. Grill her up and let her rest for about five minutes or so. While she's napping, throw a few onions on the grill (lubed up with plenty of olive oil) and let them get soft and sweet. Slice up your steak cutting across the grain, because that's what they tell us to do. And it will keep you from gnawing on your dinner like a savage. I'm a purist and need only the onions and some good guac to round it all out, but knock yourself out with all the delicious accoutrements. As you feast, just remember that one of these days we will be able to have someone bring it to us, along with enough chips and salsa to make the past several months seem ok. Until then, bon appétit, y'all!

Guess what, y'all. It's still hot and, according to our local weather dude, it's gross. Need something to delight and refresh your sorry, wilted self? Pecan crusted chicken salad will do just that. Lay your chicken breast out on a sheet of parchment and slice that girl in half horizontally. Lay another sheet on top and take out all your frustrations by pounding those girls out flat. No meat mallet? Your favorite coffee mug is happy to join the therapy session. Not only will this tenderize her, it will slenderize her, too, and shorten the time it takes for her to cook. Salt her on both sides, dredge her in a beaten egg, then in some finely chopped pecans. Press those pecans in y'all, we want maximum coverage here. In your skillet, heat up a thin layer of olive oil on medium high heat and let those girls sizzle for two to three minutes per side. Because they are so thin, the pecans are toasted to perfection at the same rate your chicken is cooked. Everybody wins. After a quick rest, slice her up and lay her out on your greens. Now add to the party whatever floats your culinary boat. I went with sliced honeycrisp apple and a stinky Stilton, but berries and chèvre or pear and shaved manchego would make your eyes roll back, too. An apple cider vinaigrette would round this out nicely, but I actually ate it au naturale, as the flavor and texture profiles were delightful all by themselves. So, until it is less gross outside, we will distract ourselves with something cool and refreshing. Bon appétit, y'all.

When we have surplus tomatoes, we can't let those beauties go to waste, so we make tomato pie, y'all. And when you don't have a traditional pie crust on hand, you pull the puff pastry out of the freezer and put her to work. In your pie plate (or cast iron skillet), lay out your dough, trim to size, and poke the bottom with a fork like you mean it. Those tine marks will keep it from puffing up too much as it bakes. Slide it into a 350° oven for about 20 minutes or until just golden. As it bakes, slice your tomatoes and sprinkle with a little salt and let her shed some of her water weight-we don't need a watery pie, y'all. Once the shell has cooled, layer up all that garden beauty and sprinkle on the cheese of your choice (of course, I went with chèvre). Next, mix together a couple of glops of mayonnaise and mounds of the cheese of your choice (I went with Parmesan). Top the 'maters with the mayo mix and pop into the oven until the top is golden and bubbly. Here's the hardest part, y'all-let it rest for about 15 minutes to let the whole thing set up a bit. It tastes like summer with a buttery crust, friends, and we need a little of both right now. Bon appétit, y'all!

When it's crazy hot outside we need a cool, crisp salad to end the week, and my "Friday salad" is just the thing. Years ago when I was an intern (and a grad student with limited means) at the Museum of Fine Arts, Houston, I would brown bag it all week so that on Fridays I could go to a local cafe and splurge. This salad was my choice every time and I still enjoy it and the fond memories associated with it on a Friday afternoon. Iceberg lettuce, shrimp, avocado, kalamata olives, slivers of red onion, and shaved Parmesan come together in a beautiful and tasty summer symphony. Bonus points because it is straight up assembly-no need for a single heat-emitting appliance to dampen the mood on a hot day! This mix is best with a creamy Caesar or buttermilk ranch, but when I'm feeling my southern girl roots, a squeeze of lemon juice and a small dollop of Hellmann's or Duke's is divine. As always, bon appétit, y'all!

I don't know who needs to hear this, but meatballs are quite comfortable served on a cloud of ricotta cheese. They've been crying out for it my whole life, but I didn't know until I had them served that way at Vagabond Pizza in Abilene. Since I can't occupy "my" seat there and indulge in all of their delights on a regular basis, I've had to concoct my own version (with a few slight modifications) here at home. Start with a good chunky tomato sauce and let it simmer away until nice and thick. Next, jazz up the ricotta with plenty of fresh herbs (I used finely chopped parsley and oregano) and a pinch of salt. Finally, sear those meatballs on a grill pan then bake at 350° for about 30 minutes or until cooked through. Grill some ciabatta lubed up with some olive oil then rub it down with a clove of garlic, and you've got the perfect delivery device for all of that deliciousness. Remember, friends, it doesn't matter if you lovingly craft your meatballs and tomato sauce with your own two hands or straight up purchase them-the combination is heavenly and there is NO shame in strategic shopping. If you find yourself in Abilene, get thee to Vagabond. Until then, whip this up for your hungry people and you will be a meatball hero. Bon appétit, y'all!

I love me some muscles. I mean mussels. And if they scare you as you pass the fish counter, consider this: they are ridiculously easy and insanely delicious. To completely misquote Field of Dreams, if you steam them, they will open, and then you can eat them. Start with a delicious pot liquor by sautéing some onion and garlic in a little olive oil. Once soft, dribble in a little white wine and let it bubble for a minute or so. Remember that super delicious chicken stock you put up in the freezer last time you roasted a chicken? That goes in next, along with a little chopped flat leaf parsley. While your pot liquor bubbles away, rinse your mussels. If they have a fuzzy little beard, pull it off–we want our little dudes clean-shaven. Dump them straight into your bubbling pot, cover, and let them relax and open up. A little white wine can do that for most of us, and these little dudes are no exception. Once they open up, they are done. That's it. You boil stuff, dump them in, and three minutes later, dinner is ready. Make sure you serve with a crusty baguette because that liquor is sop-worthy. And how do you go about eating them? My French family taught me to use an empty shell as "tongs" to pick the meat out. Delicious, fancy, AND you get to play with your grub. Is this a first-date food? Well, maybe not, but if you risk it and they still want to walk you to your door, then they just may be the one. Bon appétit, y'all!

Need a light, bright dinner option? Linguine with asparagus and lemon are the perfect option for a quick and tasty dinner! As your noodles boil away in a pot of salted water, sauté some onion and garlic (in a separate sauté pan) in a little olive oil. Once they are soft and fragrant, add the asparagus tips to that flavor party and let them get nice and cozy. Use your veggie peeler to make ribbons of the tender part of the asparagus stalk (we don't want to waste any of that green goodness) and add them to the boiling noodles for the last two minutes of cooking time. Next, squeeze the juice of one lemon into the sautéing veggies and throw in some minced parsley for good measure. Using tongs, pull the linguine and asparagus ribbons from their hot tub and plop them straight into your skillet of sizzling veggies, taking some of the starchy cooking liquid along for the ride (to help develop a silky sauce). Plate it up, then put that veggie peeler to use one more time to shave some fresh Parmesan on top. Et voilà! Bright lemon, nutty asparagus, tangy Parmesan, and linguine with just a little bite come together for pure deliciousness. Bon appétit, y'all!

Hankerin' some Asian flavor but don't want to leave the house? No problem! Just marinate thinly sliced beef in soy sauce, a tiny dribble of sesame oil, and plenty of freshly grated ginger and garlic. Park that goodness in the fridge for 30 minutes while you steam some broccoli and soak some cellophane noodles (you can find them on the same aisle as the soy sauce). Stir fry your beef in a little vegetable oil and serve with your noodles and veggies. Bonus points for topping it with sesame seeds and scallions. It's quick, easy, delicious, and you didn't even have to leave the house! Bon appétit, y'all!

Need a quick, delicious, and light lunch? Look no further than the scallop! Start by patting those beauties dry, dusting with salt, and scoring lightly to ensure they cook evenly. Next, have your stuff "mise en place" (which is just fancy for "ready to go") because the whole process happens in a flash and we do NOT want to overcook them and turn them into pencil erasers. All you need is a smidge of olive oil, a dribble of dry white wine, and fresh lemon juice. Heat the oil on high and place your scallops scored side down until they take on a bit of golden color, then flip. They are done when, to quote Annie Lennox, they turn a whiter shade of pale. Once they are opaque, they are done. Add to the skillet a splash of white wine and a generous squeeze of lemon, et voilà! In mere minutes you have sweet, tender deliciousness that is quite happy atop some angel hair pasta. An extra wedge of lemon and a sprinkle of parsley is always a good idea. Bon appétit, y'all!

Craving something bright and lemony during a global pandemic? Chicken piccata is just what we need to lift our spirits and fill our bellies. Start by pounding out your chicken between two sheets of parchment until she is slender and tender. If your breast came from a giant Godzilla chicken (like mine did) split her in half horizontally first to make your job easier. Next, salt her and dredge her in a little flour before frizzling her in a tiny bit of olive oil over medium high heat until she is bronzed and beautiful. Remove her from the pan and set her aside to catch her breath while you work on the sauce. Add your capers and a generous splash of white wine and scrape up those crunchy brown bits of flavor gold (fancy folks call this deglazing). Let the wine reduce by half. Next, add the juice of one lemon and let it bubble away for a minute or so. Finally, add a little cold butter to the mix and watch that sauce turn from yummy to "where have you been all my life" in a flash. There is some kind of strange and wonderful alchemy that happens with the addition of a little butter and I am here for it. Serve your masterpiece on a bed of angel hair, rice, or couscous because we are on a "no carb left behind" tour this year. Set it on the table and back away quickly because your hungry people will have their forks at the ready to devour all that deliciousness. Bon appétit, y'all!

In England, our Sundays were all about the roast and I still get a hankerin' for some roasty meat once Sunday rolls around. While we usually had chicken or beef, I decided to mix it up a little and opted for lamb, marinated in plenty of garlic, olive oil, lemon, and rosemary. Once she is all lubed up, park her in the fridge for a few hours. Overnight is even better. Once she's ready, shake her down a bit and remove the garlic before salting and searing her off in your cast iron skillet. In the same skillet, make a bed of similarly seasoned potatoes for her to rest on before slipping her into a 375° oven. Times will vary based on size and cut, but this shank was perfect in 35 minutes. Y'all, those potatoes with the juices raining down on them as they roast are quite smashing. Bonus British points for Yorkshire pudding, but either way, your eyes will be rolling all the way back. Bon appétit, blokes!

After celebrating all weekend with delicious junk, it's time for something light and tasty, and seared sesame tuna is IT. First, pat that ruby red beauty down with a paper towel so all the good stuff sticks. Grate some fresh (and peeled) ginger and schmear it all over her. Next, give her a gooood rub down with miso paste (thank you, Amazon pantry) and roll her around in sesame seeds. Press down well, y'all, we want maximum coverage on all sides of the steak. Get your pan screaming hot, add a dribble of vegetable oil, and let that girl sizzle. Make sure the sides have their turn, too. Once the sesame seeds are toasty, it's time to flip. Let her rest for a sec and slice away. For dipping, I like a smidge of hoisin, soy sauce, and freshly grated ginger. Y'all, we love our hot dogs, but it's time to atone for our dietary sins. Amen.

Y'all, it's hot. It's humid. And we need a little afternoon pick-me-up like nobody's business. Enter the affogato. That's just Italian for "drowned " and we are going to drown our covid mask-wearing sorrows in something easy and delicious. Scoop a little vanilla bean ice cream (anything less is a travesty), sprinkle it with a little grated dark chocolate, and top it with a shot (or two, we aren't here to judge) of hot espresso or strong coffee. Top with more chocolate because more chocolate means more happiness. I used a dark chocolate Ritter Sport bar with hazelnuts that I popped in the fridge for a bit before grating. People, given how cranky everyone is right now, this could very well SAVE LIVES! Please, do your part, y'all. And then put your mask back on. Buona sera, y'all!!

Made in the USA
Columbia, SC
09 October 2020